ZOMBIE ANIMALS
PARASITES TAKE CONTROL!

ZOMBIE CATERPILLARS

BY FRANCES NAGLE

Gareth Stevens
PUBLISHING

Please visit our website, www.garethstevens.com. For a free color catalog of all our high-quality books, call toll free 1-800-542-2595 or fax 1-877-542-2596.

Library of Congress Cataloging-in-Publication Data

Nagle, Frances, 1959- author.
  Zombie caterpillars / Frances Nagle.
      pages cm. — (Zombie animals : parasites take control!)
  Includes bibliographical references and index.
  ISBN 978-1-4824-2832-2 (pbk.)
  ISBN 978-1-4824-2833-9 (6 pack)
  ISBN 978-1-4824-2834-6 (library binding)
  1. Caterpillars—Behavior—Juvenile literature. 2. Parasitic wasps—Behavior—Juvenile literature. 3. Host-parasite relationships—Juvenile literature. 4. Parasitism—Juvenile literature. I. Title.
  QL544.2.N34 2016
  595.7813'92—dc23

                                        2014048061

First Edition

Published in 2016 by
Gareth Stevens Publishing
111 East 14th Street, Suite 349
New York, NY 10003

Copyright © 2016 Gareth Stevens Publishing

Designer: Nicholas Domiano
Editor: Kristen Rajczak

Photo credits: Cover, pp. 1, 5 Scott Camazine/Science Source/Getty Images; p. 7 Steve Hatch/Bugwood.org/Invasive.org; p. 9 Kallista Images/Getty Images; p. 11 Brian G. Green/ National Geographic/Getty Images; p. 13 José Lino-Neto/Wikimedia Commons; p. 15 Richard Bartz/Wikimedia Commons; p. 17 Noonan Robert/Science Source/Getty Images; p. 19 Photo Researchers/Getty Images; p. 21 Jktu_21/Shutterstock.com.

Printed in the United States of America

CPSIA compliance information: Batch #CS15GS: For further information contact Gareth Stevens, New York, New York at 1-800-542-2595.

CONTENTS

Words in the glossary appear in **bold** type the first time they are used in the text.

CATERPILLAR CONQUEST

What if you were **infected** by something that made it so you couldn't move? You surely wouldn't like if someone else controlled your body either! In nature, some living things don't have a choice. Gypsy moth caterpillars can get a virus that makes them act strangely and die. Other kinds of caterpillars face wasps from the animal group called *Glyptapanteles* (glihp-tuh-PAN-tuh-leez). The wasps turn caterpillars into bodyguards for their young.

Both the virus and the wasps are parasites. Their take-overs are like something from a zombie movie!

This gypsy moth would never have made it to adulthood if it was infected with a parasitic virus when it was still a larva! Caterpillars are the larvae of moths and butterflies.

TAKE-OVER TRUTHS

A PARASITE IS A LIVING THING THAT LIVES IN OR ON ANOTHER LIVING THING, OR HOST. THE PARASITE USES THE HOST AS FOOD OR IN OTHER WAYS THAT BENEFIT THE PARASITE AND OFTEN HURT THE HOST.

WICKED WASPS

In recent years, scientists have been studying *Glyptapanteles* to find out how these parasitic wasps work. There are hundreds of **species** of wasps within *Glyptapanteles*, and they are mostly found in North America and Central America.

Like other wasps, *Glyptapanteles* are insects with three main body parts, six legs, and two sets of wings. Another body part called an ovipositor is found on the back end of their body. It helps mother wasps do a very important job: lay eggs in the bodies of caterpillars!

TAKE-OVER TRUTHS

GLYPTAPANTELES IS ONLY ONE GROUP OF PARASITIC WASP. HOWEVER, OTHER KINDS DON'T MAKE ZOMBIES OUT OF THEIR HOSTS.

The caterpillar of *Chrysodeixis chalcites*, or the tomato looper moth, is just one kind of caterpillar that parasitic wasps are on the lookout for.

LAYING THE EGGS

When a female wasp is ready to lay her eggs, she sticks her ovipositor into the side of a caterpillar. Some use **venom** to **paralyze** the caterpillar so up to 80 eggs can be laid inside its body. The eggs **hatch**, and the wasp larvae begin to eat the caterpillar! They grow inside their host and shed their exoskeleton, or the outer covering on their body.

The larvae don't eat the most important parts of the caterpillar. They need the caterpillar to stay alive!

TAKE-OVER TRUTHS

SOME PLANTS, SUCH AS CABBAGE, SEND OUT CHEMICALS WHEN THERE'S A CATERPILLAR ON THEM. A WASP MAY RECOGNIZE THESE CHEMICALS IN THE AIR AND HEAD TO THE PLANT TO LAY HER EGGS.

The word "ovipositor" means "egg placer." This image shows another kind of parasitic wasp using her ovipositor to lay eggs in a gypsy moth caterpillar.

A NASTY EXIT

Glyptapanteles larvae fill up the inside of the caterpillar, making it look very fat. When the larvae have grown enough, they eat a hole through the caterpillar and make their way out. It looks pretty gross! Scientists think the wasp larvae time their final **molt** to when they're leaving the caterpillar. Their exoskeletons plug up the holes in the caterpillar's side.

Then, the larvae find a leaf or twig nearby and make cocoons. This is where they'll **develop** into adult wasps.

TAKE-OVER TRUTHS

GLYPTAPANTELES DON'T KILL TOO MANY CATERPILLARS BECAUSE ANOTHER KIND OF PARASITIC WASP PREYS ON *GLYPTAPANTELES*. THESE WASPS LAY THEIR EGGS ON *GLYPTAPANTELES* LARVAE OR COCOONS!

Parasitic wasp larvae have made their cocoons on the outside of the tomato hornworm caterpillar. However, this caterpillar will die soon—it won't become a zombie like *Glyptapanteles* make of their hosts!

ZOMBIE GUARDS

Caterpillars are supposed to eat! They also molt, grow, and make cocoons in which they develop into adult moths. However, when *Glyptapanteles* larvae have left a caterpillar's body, the caterpillar's purpose changes. Once the larvae have made cocoons, the caterpillar stops eating and moving. It's now a zombie bodyguard!

Glyptapanteles larvae in their cocoons have many predators, such as stinkbugs. If a predator nears the cocoons, the caterpillar rears up and starts swinging its head around to scare the bug away!

Caterpillars only act this way when guarding cocoons of *Glyptapanteles*.

TAKE-OVER TRUTHS

STUDIES HAVE SHOWN THAT WASP COCOONS GUARDED BY ZOMBIE CATERPILLARS WERE TWICE AS LIKELY TO SURVIVE AS UNGUARDED COCOONS.

WHAT'S GOING ON?

There are a few ideas about how the host caterpillar becomes a zombie to guard the cocoons. First, the mother wasp may pass on a **gene** to the caterpillar when she lays her eggs. It would make parts of the caterpillar's body stop working so her young would be safe inside it.

Other studies say a few larvae don't leave the caterpillar's body with the rest. They may stay behind to control the caterpillar while their brothers and sisters develop in the cocoons.

TAKE-OVER TRUTHS

THE WASPS LEFT BEHIND IN THE CATERPILLAR ARE GIVING UP THEIR OWN LIVES SO THEIR SPECIES CAN KEEP SURVIVING.

All caterpillars that are hosts to parasitic wasps, like this one, die once the adult wasps leave their cocoons.

INFECTED!

Not much is grosser than the thought of a caterpillar turning to goo and dripping onto the forest floor below! But that's exactly what happens to caterpillars infected with a certain virus. This virus has a gene that turns caterpillars into zombies!

Uninfected gypsy moth caterpillars are happy to climb trees and munch on leaves at night. In the morning, they come back down to hide. Those with the virus, however, go up and never come down.

TAKE-OVER TRUTHS

THE VIRUS GENE *THAT* MAKES CATERPILLARS INTO ZOMBIES IS CALLED *EGT*.

Gypsy moth caterpillars don't climb trees during the day because they could be seen by birds and other insects that like to eat them.

IT'S CATCHING

Gypsy moth caterpillars often get the virus from other infected caterpillars! The virus forces the caterpillars to climb trees during the day, instead of at night. It also stops them from molting. Caterpillars eat a lot before they molt, and the virus wants them to keep eating. The more a caterpillar grows, the more the virus can grow inside it!

The caterpillar stays up in the tree until it dies. Then, the virus turns it to liquid, which drips to leaves below. Other caterpillars eat these leaves, and the **cycle** begins again!

Scientists first saw this strange caterpillar **behavior** about 100 years ago.

TAKE-OVER TRUTHS

A BIRD COULD HELP SPREAD THE VIRUS BY BITING INTO AN INFECTED CATERPILLAR AND SPRAYING ITS LIQUID INSIDES! A BIRD'S WASTE COULD ALSO CONTAIN THE VIRUS FROM CATERPILLARS IT'S EATEN.

USING PARASITES

Caterpillars and the moths they grow into are often seen as pests. Some harm crops by feeding on them. People want to use both *Glyptapanteles* and the gypsy moth virus to control their populations.

Scientists are trying to figure out ways to make the same chemicals plants do to draw the wasps to places where too many caterpillars are feeding. People are also hoping to use the gypsy moth virus to stop the caterpillars, which can quickly overpopulate.

GYPSY MOTH POPULATION GROWTH

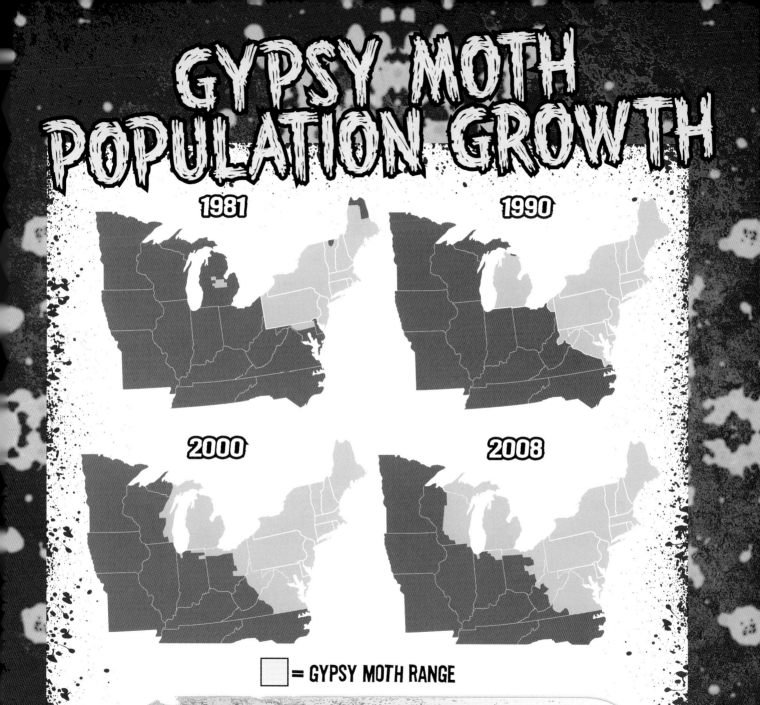

1981

1990

2000

2008

☐ = GYPSY MOTH RANGE

Using the virus to control gypsy moth caterpillar overpopulation is seen as better for other animals and plants than pesticides, or chemicals made to kill insects.

GLOSSARY

behavior: the way an animal acts

chemical: matter that can be mixed with other matter to cause changes

cycle: a series of occurrences that happen over and over

develop: to grow and change

gene: a tiny part of a cell that is passed along from one living thing to its offspring

hatch: to break open or come out of

infect: to pass on an illness

molt: the act of losing an outer covering

paralyze: to make something lose the ability to move

prey: to hunt animals for food

species: a group of plants or animals that are all the same kind

venom: a poison made inside an animal's body

FOR MORE INFORMATION

BOOKS

Johnson, Rebecca L. *Zombie Makers: True Stories of Nature's Undead.* Minneapolis, MN: Millbrook Press, 2013.

Trueit, Trudi Strain. *Caterpillars and Butterflies.* New York, NY: Marshall Cavendish Benchmark, 2011.

WEBSITES

Photo Gallery: Real Zombies
*www.cbc.ca/natureofthings/features/
photo-gallery-real-zombies*
Check out information and photos of all kinds of zombie animals, including the caterpillar.

Zombie Caterpillar
*www.smithsonianmag.com/videos/category/wildlife/
zombie-caterpillar/?no-ist*
Watch a video of a zombie caterpillar keeping predators away from the wasps living inside it.

Publisher's note to educators and parents: Our editors have carefully reviewed these websites to ensure that they are suitable for students. Many websites change frequently, however, and we cannot guarantee that a site's future contents will continue to meet our high standards of quality and educational value. Be advised that students should be closely supervised whenever they access the Internet.

INDEX